When I Looked Back You Were Gone

Poems by

Cary Waterman

HOLY COW! PRESS • DULUTH, MINNESOTA • 1992

ISBN 0-930100-47-6
Library of Congress Number: 92-52505

Photograph of Cary Waterman by Amy Waterman
Cover: Handtinted photograph by Mary McDunn, "Sybil" (Homage Series)

Publisher's Address:
Holy Cow! Press
Post Office Box 3170
Mount Royal Station
Duluth, Minnesota

Distributor's Address:
The Talman Company, Inc.
150 Fifth Avenue
New York, New York 10011

This project is supported, in part, by a grant from the National Endowment for the
Arts in Washington, D.C., a Federal Agency.

Acknowledgments

Some of these poems have been previously published in the following magazines: *Connecticut River Review, Green Mountain Review, Labyris, The Literary Review, Loonfeather, Milkweed Chronicle, Minnesota Times, Nimrod, Northeast Journal, Painted Bride Quarterly, Primavera, Poetry Now, Rag Mag, The Roundtable, The Webster Review, The Wooster Review,* and *Yarrow*.

"Last Game" appeared in the anthology, *This Sporting Life, (Milkweed Editions)*. "Raising Lambs" appeared in the anthology, *The Decade Dance, (Sandhills Press)*.

The author wishes to thank the Bush Foundation and the Minnesota State Art Board for fellowships which made possible the writing of many of these poems. She would also like to thank The Loft and the McKnight Foundation for their generous support.

The author also would like to thank the MacDowell Colony and the Tyrone Guthrie Centre in appreciation for the time she spent in residency.

Many thanks also to Kate Green and Roseann Lloyd for midwifing this book into print.

for Amy, Bridgit, and Devin
who have always been faithful

Table of Contents

III

TO FREE THEM ALL

"Whoever you are, no matter how lonely,
the world offers itself to your imagination,
calls to you like the wild geese, harsh and exciting—
over and over announcing your place
in the family of things."

— Mary Oliver
from *"Wild Geese"*

I

WHAT IS IN THE BODY AND WHAT IS NOT

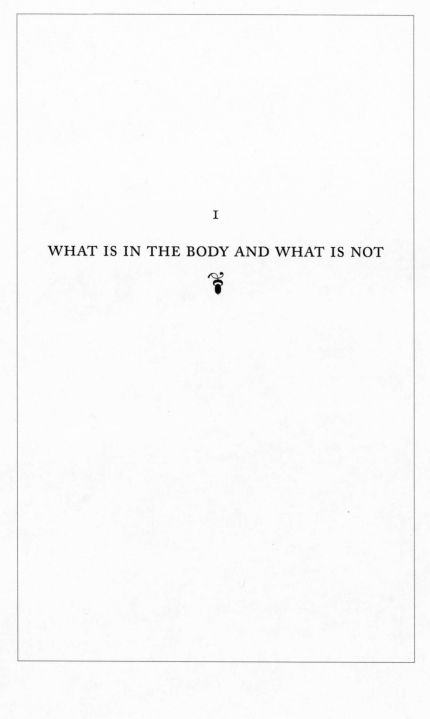

THE NEW LANGUAGE

I cannot say how amazed I am to think of you so far away.
I wake up this morning and know you are in Asia,
your plane set down on foreign tarmac with you
peering from a small window.

Two days ago you were here in your old childhood bed,
your head turned to the blue Minnesota sky.
This morning you are gone, tinkling new silver coins in your pockets.
You are farther away from me who was your belly-money,
than you have ever been before.

I remember when you began your long stroke away from me,
the cheek of the pond that winter day smooth and cold.
It seemed like you were born knowing life was an icicle
that had to be sucked down to its sharpest point
before it disappeared entirely under the melt of tongue.

You were the child who would not stay put,
who would go anywhere and was chased down again and again
through neighbors' backyards and across busy intersections.
When you were three you followed the high school marching band
down the street and back into the gymnasium.
More than once you rode home in the back seat of a squad car,
your tricycle propped up beside you.
I scolded and spanked but it did no good.

You have been chasing the sun.
Last night you crossed six thousand miles of water wilderness,
with no mother to guide you.

The light of the East appeared and hovered on the ocean's rim.
Today you begin the heartstrokes of Chinese,
a breath and then the soft black line that glides you into speech.
It seemed I only turned away one second.
A silver pencil of plane lifted you into the physics of wind and wing.
When I looked back you were gone.

NIGHT RAIN

I

Trying to pry my eyes up
I see you standing by the bed
straight as a wind funnel.
You wake me into the storm,
lightning and thunder beating
on the doors of your eyes.
We roll up in bed together,
a doughnut and the doughnut hole.
We pull into this burrow
all the small facts of love.

II

I find this bit of words
years later. Now
I cannot even remember
which one you were.
Daughter? Son?
Which one came on that night
down the wilderness of stairs,
woke me hard from my sleep?
Which one of you was it
that needed my body?

And at what click of
your own timebomb
did you go splashing off
into fearlessness,
leaving old records, data,
your own small fossils
embedded in my skin?

CROCUS

One crocus in bloom suddenly.
I find it on the shelf beside
my bed with its sprawled sheets
and the empty clothes left
breathless on the floor.
This flower of resurrection,
forced through the hard soil of a pot,
has come stabbing into air.
It is purple and gloved
like many hands, one folded
on the other, covering the secret
night birth, the sound of quick breaths
not able to be held.

Now it is here,
first flower of spring
which you have given to me.
And how easy it is to wait
for the rest, accepting
the shortness of this life
which is persistent,
to be counted on,
like the sun that comes this morning
filtered through white curtains
that separate, but only slightly,
what is in the body
and what is not.

HOME MOVIES

The audience vanishes into upholstered chairs.
In a dark room family actors
move across the bubbled snow of screen.
Mother, father, my brother at seven,
his small dark bathing suit silhouetted
like the wingspan of a bat against
the backdrop of a Long Island sand dune.

We both got sunburned that day.
At night our mother laid us on our stomachs
on the living room floor, white-washing us
with the chalky cold of refrigerated
Milk of Magnesia, a housewives' cure
for our burning shoulders and backs.
It didn't matter.
We blistered anyway.

The last frames of childhood
slip off the spoked wheel.
The reel rotates slower and slower,
and the loose film flaps,
once, twice, three times,
until someone's hand catches it,
reaches up, turns off the projector light.

The audience does not move,
stunned by this emptiness.
We had left our bodies for those on the screen.
Now we come pouring back into ourselves

the way you scoop up a shovelful of sand
and pour it into a burlap bag
which will be piled on a hundred other bags
to make a wall to hold back the flood.

Then we begin to move.
The heavy clothes. Stiff legs.
Feet that had gone to sleep
are massaged awake.
We rub our eyes to wipe away
the other life.
Then someone stands,
snaps up the shade.

THE VISIT

Connecticut, August, 1985

My mother's backyard.
I sit at the old yellow umbrella table,
and wait for it to happen.
Cicadas unfurl their usual August racket.
Again this year, the neighbors have not
cleaned or filled their backyard pool.
Weeds have sprouted in the collected mulch
of the deep end.
Traffic in the street has increased drone by drone
a hundred times since I was last here.
At the corner stop sign, brakes give
the screechiest of whines.

This time I have come back here with my three
nearly adult children and my man-friend.
His bathing suit clutches the clothesline over my head,
hanging between my suit and our old family beach towels.
One towel has shells on it. The other, a Budweiser can.
The third is monogrammed in black with my initials.
It has two flamingos, one looking at the other
who has bent to peck away the A of my middle name,
which was also the name of my favorite aunt
who lies in a graveyard near here
buried under a massive Celtic Cross.

I come back again and again to these beginnings,
an exile ricochetting between the future and the past.
In the house next door the widow who was my mother's friend
has died. When her day came
they wheeled her out to a waiting ambulance,
fiery in its haste to be off.
Now her bushes pull their shadows
up under them for the night.
The cicadas sing and sing.
Our old towels hang again into the dark.

SKATING THE CREEK

We skated for miles that day,
the creek a clear transparent thought
twisting around the brown banks
that held us in and hugged us
like the long arms of some inexhaustible mother.
This was the first smooth ice of winter,
a testimony to the invisible cold
that came at night and burrowed in
around our windows and doors.
Embedded in the ice there were only
bits of leaf scrap,
or a single owl's feather drifted down
to mark the creek like a flower laid
on someone's frozen grave.

We took the ice together,
Bridgit, Amy, and Devin, the youngest,
on twin-bladed skates that were
like little sleds for his small feet.
This frozen water was the boundary line
between two fields brittle
in their unrelieved death.
Bare trees and summer vines
were crushed in a brown embrace.
And on the steep banks we found
the footprints of something small,
a message scribbled from one side to the other.

The creek seemed to go on forever
with us skating, skating,
climbing over fallen trees
that were like withered arms
set out to hold us back.
There was some singing in this ice.
And there were places where the frozen water
cracked as we went over,
like a rifle shot into the cold afternoon.
But it was all behind us,
the place we crossed seconds ago
only now shifting
in memory of our weight.

What did we seek out there,
pulled as we were by some invisible thread?
We skated on, the creek demanding that we always
go further, and our own desires stroking
down our legs like fire to see
again and again what was beyond the next bend.
It was always just another bend.
We knew there was only more of the same.
But all of it was different.
The frozen hands of the trees.
The brown saplings, tearless in the ice.
We were new at every turn and
every straight-away as we pushed further on,
the water's icy tongue a memory
suspended underneath our moving life.
It held us up.

That day we did not reach the end.
It was too far for us to travel on silver blades,
to go all the way to the mouth of that creek
where it met the river and began
its long run down the birth canal
to the blue-bellied sea.
We turned back,
only having gone that far together,
my children in their quilted snowsuits,
their sweet, wishbone legs playing over the frozen water
like bows on a violin.
Underneath us, all the small things
were burrowed in for the winter,
things saved for us,
etched into our memories
all along the way back.

DIVORCE

In my dream I could not
get the poem to fit its page.
This is the way sometimes
I do not know who we are.

Today in the late afternoon light
I saw how tires of cars
made trapezoids in the snow,
the lines cut perfectly as if
to frame a diminishing face.

And tonight my son would not go
with his father, did not want to see
the sweat and pull of young men wrestling.
Instead he sat by me for a while.
Then went to play Dungeons and Dragons,
another world where people do not marry or divorce,
where there is no sex,
no failing.

THE MOTHERS

for Susan

> *"Bright, slender necked*
> *Dandelion on stalk—*
> *I can't fully grasp*
> *That my child is in earth."*
> *—Marina Tsvetayeva*

A death inside everything—
trees, window curtains, the flash
of bike rammed into a truck.
And his young head is replaced
by another. And then another.
You tell me you believed you could
pull him back if you held
that dead hand long enough,
tried hard enough.
We have all needed
to believe this.

Now you wear your old totem clothes,
mourning shawl, wooden skirt,
and join the mothers of the dead.
The one who after two abortions
found her son breathless in his crib.
The mother of the leukemia child
watching the blood erupt under baby skin.
The mother of the swollen body
at the bottom of the swimming pool.
The mother of the one crumpled by the road
covered with a blanket.

When I reach home tonight my children
will be safe, sleeping in their dark beds.
I'll lock the doors, the windows,
leave a lamp to shine against death
who is dressed in a cape of many pockets.

Sealing Up

The house is a mess of cold
like an egg cracked in the night.
Winter leaks in everywhere,
coming sneaky.
We feel the draft but
cannot find the fault
that lets it in.

Outside, snow.
At least it stays there.
But the wind creeps and snuggles
through every separation.
The cracked glass of mirrors.
A split in the fingernail.
The space between hairs on our arms.

It keeps us honest,
will not let us be fooled too long
by the lie of warmth.
Birds at the feeder
are frantic in this weather,
their little helicopter bodies
tilting, tossed.

I light a fire,
such momentary flames,
and think of the graveyard dead
buried in leaded tombs,

in satin with plump pillows
for their heads.
I go to seal things up.
But it is no use.
It will all come in
no matter what lies,
what fabrications are pasted
to windows, doors.

FEEDING THE CAT

for K.D.

I

This mother is sick.
Get milk from the icebox.
Listen to her sticky tits.
And she coughs, chokes
on her own life.

But how she loves those kittens
sucking her dry.
Loves them enough
to let them pin her to the floor
in a sculpture of maternity.

She takes in air, food,
and gives it out again
like a country mailbox,
the small door of her,
the tired hinge opens
and opens and opens again.

II

I dream about
the no-name cat,
dream she is spitting out sickness
on the couch where I sleep.

She has come into my dream
like a knife.
She cuts toward me through
my own darkness,
howls me awake,
and makes me cry.

I want to put her to sleep,
fill her with the novocaine of night,
send her into death's garden.

III

I am filled with
the beautiful pain of fall.
My children grow away from me,
away from the summer's fire.
It is the same every year.
Like a dying star
I want to keep all their light.

On this long night before winter
the cat wanders like a silent thought
through the house.
She comes to rub against my leg,
to curl up beside me.
We know we love what smothers us,
love the thin air,
and wait for a sleeve of snow
to soften boundary lines,
conceal the fields of separation.

RENTERS

Someone has lived here before me,
a girl with her lover.
I find her hair, long and heavy,
slowing the drain in the bathtub.
I find empty gift boxes,
left-behind clothes.
She pressed into him here
night after night.
Then he went back to his wife.

Why do we love each other?
Why hold flesh
in momentary light?
Outside maples are turning,
burning. They dazzle me
with their essential death.

She is still here
in this third floor room,
this nest, this high place.
We pace each other,
leave bits of ourselves
across the air,
clues for those
who will follow.
I find her skin cream
cobwebbed in a corner.
I find her diminishing soap.

THE BAT IN THE BEDROOM

I woke in thick black
to the rhythmic smash into window shades
beyond which was the great December dark.
I thought they slept all winter,
curled mothers and babies
tucked into eaves.
I pulled the covers over my head,
wished the cat to come,
sit on the bed,
see me through until dawn.

This morning the bat hung
from a window cornice.
A large bat, upside down,
with feet like tiny pitchforks
that seemed to sniff the air
and help her tell light from dark,
the real from the imagined.
She was patient while I dressed,
listening for the knock of my forgotten dreams.
She heard me slip past her, close the door,
take all that dark energy with me.

The whole day things went wrong.
Cars veered into my lane and hung there,
swinging back just at the last moment.
In offices men told me gibberish while I watched
dark bow ties tilt and wiggle under their chins.
And at a party I turned suddenly,
wine flying like laughter out of my glass
and down someone's back.

When I got home the bat was still there,
hanging on, waiting.
I got the tennis racket. I got a towel.
I got a big shoe finally and did it,
not knowing what else to do.
I put the body in a snowbank outside the back door.
Then I waited,
held my arms out from my sides,
listened for the lift of wind.

THE DANCE

We fall asleep with our sweaters on.
You are the man I have looked for
beyond the mirror, your arms
like light on water.
Dark pine and spruce ring this bed
as if it were a pond where
the night animals move toward us to drink
brushing their musky fur against
needles and star points.

We are cradled all night
at the top of my old house from which
smoke rises in a column of prayer.
We do not hear or dream the knives
of the afternoon.
But in this room your mother
dances in the corner,
a slow narcotic rising from her ankles.
Her housedress sways while we drift.
Her body like loon wings folds
into itself.

That I love you does not
preclude this sorrow.
You are quiet in my arms as your mother turns,
the gardenia slipping from her hair.
Your father's rings pull heavy on her fingers.
I hear them distantly clink against each other.
Army rings. Madness rings.
The ring of the soup kettle.
The final ring of darkness.

THE CUT

For days after it happened, any small excuse would split my thumb open again. A bump against the car steering wheel. A sharp gesture toward the light. Those two small lips cut into my flesh by the life of a jagged can lid would howl and cry blood again. Bandaids were not much use since the wound was in what we have always known was an awkward place.

Friends on whom I bled counseled stitches to hold the skin together, against its will. But I waited, not wanting the introduction of black x's, a swastika of thread, the look of something patched. And not wanting also that additional pain of the needle, for which they charge by the stitch, $8 each. But most of all, I did not want the sitting in the antiseptic waiting room with all the other broken, bleeding ones comparing the quality of our blood and the fine, ecstatic singing of our pain.

It healed itself, my thumb. I forgot it, and one evening after a day of work I looked and there it was, strong and sassy, sticking up like a miniature obelisk, a model Washington Monument in pink female flesh. It had some dirt on it, some ink stains. And a scab running through the lines of my skin, going all the way across in a little grin, nonchalantly, like nothing much had happened to all those happy cells. No Sherman's March through Georgia. No Red Sea. Only the black-blood seam. And weeks later there is just a tenderness, a momentary reminder when without thinking I rub my finger against the tip of my thumb and feel the merest suggestion of scar.

TIME

I call the hospital room in Iowa where my children's grandmother answers with a shaky voice. Here in Minneapolis it is raining. If we were outside standing in the rain and crying no one would know.

I call this woman I have known for a quarter of a century and whom I love terribly even though I am no longer married to her son. Phone wires spin as she grieves old age, the failing body, the slowness.

When the sunlight comes, it is over twenty-five years of water surrounding my two daughters paddling there on a slow afternoon. Grandmother behind us on a blanket sets out sandwiches and grape juice. The girls splash, then run for the food and the thick towels she wraps around each one.

It is summer. Flowers drink this rain we're having. Then they lean, heavy, blooming, toward the earth.

AT FORTY-SIX

You've just left the interstate.
So far it's been a very long drive.

Now you're on a two-lane country road.
Sometimes there's a snaky yellow line.

Sometimes just a lot of dashes.
You're heading west and the sun is going down.

The car runs smoothly, purring almost,
and you appreciate that.

Other drivers, one by one, turn their headlights on.
They're all going the other way.

You see the red eyes of their cars
grow smaller in your rear view mirror.

Set back from the road are old white farmhouses
that haven't been painted for a long time.

Some of the windows are boarded up
and it doesn't look like anyone's around.

Just then a car coming toward you strays
the slightest bit over the center line.

Then it moves back.
It's getting darker all the time

and the radio is playing that old song,
"Heartaches, heartaches,
you'll never know how much my heart aches."

Overhead there's a shelf of dirt-grey clouds.
But in the west you can still see

the big red throb of sun going down.
The little windows of your odometer

are just about to turn 82,000 miles.
You don't know if there's time left

to drive like hell on the chance
that you can still catch it

or whether it's too late
to do anything about it at all.

A TYPOLOGY OF SAD

It's sad to be alive in this world where oil soaked otters are fished from the icy waters off Alaska.

And it must be sad to be the wildlife specialist who has to identify the black, limp carcasses and even I who have only a little TV can tell how awful it is and know that someone should pay for those deaths. But not money.

It's sad there isn't a penance, that the guilty don't have to walk in bare feet over the rocks like the Irish pilgrims at Lough Derg, which is also called Purgatory. The rocks would tear their skin and mark the ground with blood, extracting a punishment for the family of otters.

It's sad those sinners won't spend fifteen days fasting and then be locked in a cave overnight so that the real demons can come. On the sixteenth morning they would fall on their knees before the oil-soaked bodies.

It's sad this will not happen. It's business as usual in the boardrooms across America. The columns line up. Assets. Debits.

The dead ones roll over in an oily sea, one eye to the sun, one to the dark below.

BEDS

In the photo I look lovely. I am seven or eight standing with my grandparents at the Bridgeport Railroad Station. We are going to visit my aunt and uncle in New Jersey where my cousin and I will get to sleep together in the big double bed in her absent brother's room way up on the third floor of her house and drink Hires Root Beer from glass bottles and sniff the shoe-polish brown jar on his bookcase which really stinks and is reputed to contain his extracted appendix.

I am smiling in the photo, maybe because I am young and don't know anything yet. Neither of my grandparents smiles. My grandmother has on a dress I remember, a blue one with white polka dots like a night sky filled with stars. She wears her pearls, a single strand, and a small white hat with a veil. She also has on white shoes so that we know this photo was taken after Memorial Day but before Labor Day, the only permissible time for wearing white.

My grandfather has on his straw hat, white shirt with no tie, and dark jacket. He looks like what he was, a country boy from Germany come to work in the factories of an American city. I can imagine him carrying my thin Irish grandmother off to bed, but I wonder if she ever enjoyed it. They slept in separate beds, and in separate bedrooms, all the time I knew them. In fact, he died alone in his bed—a cerebral hemorrhage in his sleep. But I know they only began to sleep apart after my mother left the house, and the other bedroom, when she got married.

My mother had always slept with her sister until my aunt eloped one night. At the time of the photo, my mother slept in a separate bed, as did my father. They had bought a set of twin maple beds when they got married. My aunt and uncle slept separately too, at least as I remember. Except that there was some talk later of "The Marriage Bed." I'm not sure which one this was, but it might have been the bed my brother ended up with after my aunt and uncle moved to Florida which was the same bed my cousin and I used to sleep in up in the sanctuary of the third floor and which was really her brother's bed but might very well have been the bed in which he was conceived.

My mother died in the bed she slept apart from my father in, but that was years after he had died. This was the same bed my daughter slept in when we visited and it was also the bed my pregnant sister-in-law slept in when we were all home for my mother's funeral except that she and my brother pushed those old twin maple beds up against each other in the big bedroom so that they could reach across to each other in the dark.

My brother and sister-in-law recently bought a new bed. He doesn't like it because he says it's too big and they don't have to hug each other anymore to keep from falling out. I just bought a new bed, too. I slept in it last night for the first time. It's also bigger than my old bed. It's queen-sized with plenty of room to spread out and my feet don't hang over the bottom. I sleep there with the two cats, one on either side.

Scientists tell us we spend one-third of our lives in bed. Do we all grow apart from each other like this, needing more and more room for our aging dreams? I was conceived in one of those narrow twin beds where my parents slept separately. That night they must have held onto each other to keep from falling. Or was it the fall that counted, the falling together on a narrow bed which is really like a short pathway to the door of your life?

II

DANCING TO THE KIVA

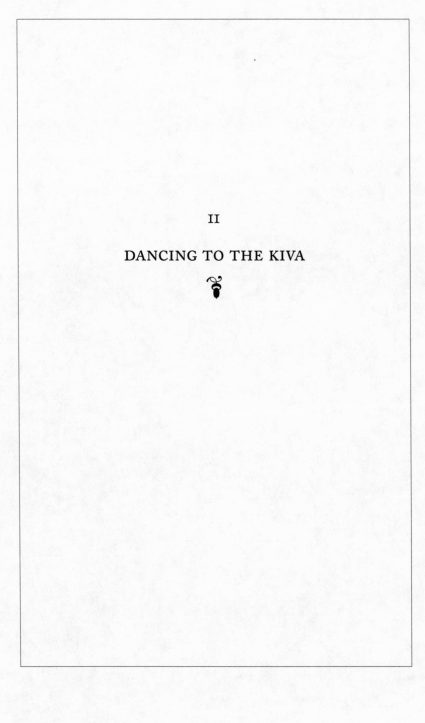

EASTER AT THE SANTA CLARA PUEBLO

We park our cars in long lines and walk down the dirt road to the center of the pueblo following an old trail of dusty boot heels. All around us are mountains, the Jemenez still snow-tipped where other Easter celebrants ski, their feet flying over the slopes like hawks' talons.

Down here we cradle the ground. This is what's real—two rows of dancers arranged, as if for a family portrait, in descending order of height. And so at the very end of the line—which is also the beginning—a little girl no more than four prepares to follow the footsteps of the one before her.

Drumming begins. It hypnotizes and makes something in me want to cry. It becomes a heartbeat, blood pounding through the veins on my skull, the pulse of my temples picking up the echoing beat of the earth. There are four hearts here—four drums—and many more singers. One drum is still unpainted, deer skin stretched like an open palm across the dark inside, the new heart that the others make room for.

The dancers face the drummers and the drums. They are all connected like sinew, like deer gut. The dancers are the arms and legs of the drumbeating heart. Up and down the small plaza in the dust of Easter Sunday, they dance for corn, for rain. They dance for us, the visitors, who have come waving our heavy limbs. They dance for the deer and the turtle. The eagle and the snake. They dance for those who have gone away and for those yet to come.

The sun warms down miles of snowy mountain trail. Someone is here who is Mother. Maiden. Old One. Crone. They dance wearing the fox tail to remind us of our beginnings. They dance carrying the offering of blue and yellow corn. They dance all the way to the Kiva before disappearing back into its womb.

CUSTOM CATTLE FEEDLOT

Hereford, Texas

Cattle almost as far as I can see.
Black and white, brown and white,
hundreds, thousands of them packed
shoulder to muscled shoulder,
standing in their own shit,
their faces like chunks of stone.
These are your steaks.
This is the prime rib,
the Sunday pot roast tied up with string,
dripping its life juices.
Our chattering minds say it's okay.
These cows could not with their combined intelligences
light up the dimmest bulb.

But they do have that for-lost look in their eyes.
Their ears curl like furred geranium leaves.
Their tongues lick each other like
the right side of sandpaper.
In a final act of will,
a few have managed to climb the little hill
of plowed-up dung and stand there,
heads above all the others gathered below them
on the diseased ground.

We pass them in the morning going north,
the wind blowing away from us.
When we return it is dark
except for the skeletons of stilted nightlights.
The cattle are lying down
and we cannot see the herd,
or the ripple that runs through it
as the wind picks up their death smell,
pushes it toward us to eat.

AT THE VIETNAM MEMORIAL

for Caroline Marshall

We look for names.
In the yellow pages of the dead
we thumb through.
Drizzle, cold, a numb day.

I do not find my names,
the men who disappeared
from my life.
This means they are still out there,
married, fathers,
gone to jobs,
to padded bars at night.
I check two times to make sure.

You find your name,
someone from high school,
and do not tell me more.
Lover? The tallest center
on the basketball team?
Look. He still stampedes
down the court, his eyes
permanent in the glare of light.
The floor-boards are slick, shiny.
And the ball released right now
from the grace of his body
goes up, over, and drops
like a severed head through the hoop.

We move down the marble gravestones.
So many, we cannot count,
we cannot help but see
our own bodies reflected,
pushed back at us darkly,
our faces tattooed with the
names of the dead.

THE BASEBALL GAME

The players are like angels
standing on a warped cross.
Young boys in white and red.
Their suits splash color
on the grass.
The pitcher aims his body
like a pistol toward the batter
who crouches now
and bobs up and down.
The catcher is all bulk
hunkered into a fist.
My son in left field
whistles silently
through his wad of gum.

I press my body against
the chainlink fence,
suspended between fathers
who gnaw at metal,
or stand rigid, silent as wood.
Then it comes,
a white rocket of leather and flame,
a speeding toy,
careening too high,
off course.
It stops where it meets
the batter's face.

Now there is blood all over
the neat uniform,
the young boy's mouth.
He goes down
like a scrap of paper.
I turn away, hands
to my face,
feel the brokenness
in those airy bodies
of boys who would be men
pinned to the green
playing field.

MILITARY FUNERAL AT LES INVALIDES

for Maureen

Drums far off. You and I are only tourists, women traveling through their own history. We have come here because my son expects a souvenir and a report on Napoleon's final resting place. There the little man lies, dreaming strategy from the catafalque while a chorus of lonely women's voices tear at his old heart. We look for Josephine who should be here, but we cannot find her. We would rather see her tomb and we check our guidebooks. She is not here.

More drums come across the cobblestones that are laid end to end with the morning rain puddled between them. Young officers appear, decorated with ribbons of one war or another. One of them carries a black pillow on which a saber and medals lie. A coffin follows, draped with the Tri-color of France. And last of all the family, old women in black veils carrying thin-leaved prayer books. Incense floats from the church of St. Louis des Invalides where Christ looks both male and female hanging below the shreds of bloody flags.

From spare, white hospital rooms toothless soldiers in wheelchairs have come to see their comrade off. They line up on the cold, wet stones. Together we watch the procession disappear across the courtyard. Together we watch the rolling up of flags. Then an old one smiles at you, winks, breaks the death of this moment. In his dreams you have met before, down by the Seine or lingering over wine on the Ile de la Cité where he held your hands, brushed his lips to your ear, whispered closely, intimately of war.

CHICAGO LOVE POEM

Snow-coated horses clop through the streets
six floors beneath us pulling
their black-wheeled tourist carriages
while we who have risen up in an airy hotel elevator
make love like two gun-blue whales,
one turning in over the other.
Outside snow falls down between
slabs of skyscrapers.
We roll and float away
over the luminous Wrigley Building,
over the Sears Tower,
scraping our great fins on the red amaryllis.
We float over Lake Michigan where yesterday
three fishermen were lost,
their bodies embraced for all time
in the tireless arms of water.
And I say how I still love the way
you come to hold me after all this time,
the way our bodies fit,
a white message in an envelope.
And how astounding it is that we still
rise above the dark mass of the city
and above our own deaths
to hold together where sky meets shore
and the land falls away
as if down a galaxy of blossoms.

PORTHMADOG, WALES

At dusk we saw thrushes gathering
in the black lace trees.
Now I am the only one
to wake in the Welsh night
to their singing,
high, clear water-notes
as if they were the voices
of young girls with shawls
under the cold Irish Sea.
I have been dreaming of marriage again.
And I have been dreaming of failure.

Yesterday we climbed
the surviving towers of Caernarvon.
Over our heads families of gulls
wheeled in from the sea.
Now, at the back of this narrow house
you and I sag toward each other
in the double bed, my son
beside us on a cot.
You are a childless man
and you sleep beside me,
comforting and not comforting,
holding and letting go
like the clasp on an old locket.
Inside the faces of many children
are hidden.

In the morning the husband of this house
will serve us breakfast.
He will come from behind the kitchen door
bearing the dead weight of full platters.
We will only hear his wife
singing and clattering her pots and pans
in the morning liturgy.
Porridge. Eggs. A slab of blood pudding.
On the walls around us
photographs of their children
will scatter like buckshot.

ANTIGONE IN ARMAGH, NORTHERN IRELAND

for Bernard and Mary Laughlin

At night we cross the border,
pass through no-man's land,
a lonely strip abandoned to crickets
and the persistence of hard-luck sheep.
We stop at the sentry post, blinded
like deer with a sudden yellow spotlight.
Inside the concrete bunker
some young, angry soldier from Liverpool
or the rancid London slums
checks our license plate on his computer.
He signals us to enter.
We never see him.
We do see the spikes
embedded in the road
that can with the flick of his hand
sink breathless into tires
of more suspicious cars.

In Armagh,
city of twin hills with twin cathedrals
that growl at each other across
the dense valley air,
we hear Antigone pledge once again
to honor her brother's death.
Isme, obedient and afraid,
will fail her.
Creon, seduced by power,
will fail also.
In the blind, mistaken purposes of state
this house will fall.

Driving home through the misted Irish countryside,
rain moves in.
Thatches and roses fly by us.
It is easy to believe we are safe
inside this innocent, non-political car.
As safe as the sheep wandering
back and forth across the border,
sheep with the red kiss
of owners on their fleece,
tearing the impartial grass.

SUNDAY MORNING: BRUSSELS

From the train window everything is flat, deserted.
Long, pale tongues of autobahns
slicken in the dawn light.
It has rained,
and the rain touched everything
with its feeling of despair.

It is not time yet
for the Sunday morning church-going.
Or for the small claustrophobic family dinners.
So it is easy to imagine an army
marching through here,
the scarred weave of tank-tread,
the precise lines of a black swastika
fluttering, the morning splintered
into death.

It would be untrue to say now
that nothing is here.
And yet on this rainy Sunday morning
that is what it is like.
We pass through unnoticed,
the gentle curve of rails,
the train cars flowing together down to the docks.
Oostende. The end of land.

In the station a silence says
there is no reason to go any further.
Two English punks done up in black suits
take snapshots of nothing much.
Perhaps it is that Sundays are always like this,
the day when you cannot move forward or backward,
the day when things stand still except
for the occasional sound of water
splashing into an enameled sink
and the silent rise of steam
from a tureen of long-simmered soup.

PHOTOGRAPH OF THE CHILDREN OF IZIEU

"Forty-five children rounded up at the village of Izieu sang in happy innocence as they rode away in trucks to Nazi extermination camps where all but one would be killed."

> —Minneapolis Tribune
> May 28, 1987

They are eight, nine, ten.
It is hard to tell.
The trees behind them are much older.
And the chest high stone wall that keeps them in.
They will not live as long
as any of these things.
Not even as long as this spring
which rips through their childhood
like scissors through a bolt of white cloth.

One boy turns his head away
from the camera.
Perhaps someone behind him has called out his name.
Or maybe he only turns
to watch the orioles soar and dive,
the veins of his neck pulled taut
like the twisted roots of a pear tree.
He is thin,
the least nourished of all of them,
and so the child who has begun first
down the slide to death.
The sun pours around him.

All the others face front and smile.
The one with the dark balloon
floating like an eclipsed sun
on a string above his head.
And the one with two black sockets for eyes.
Perhaps he is the child who was saved
because he was not Jewish.
Or perhaps it is the one who poses,
who throws open his arms
as if he would introduce himself to the world
and then dance,
the legs of his striped prison pants
fluttering from him.

AT THE CHICAGO ZOO

for Ellen Thomson

In the mammal house the old orangutan
has seen it all before:
the sick, the crazies,
the poor wrinkled ones as brittle
as onionskin.
For them the gorilla is elegant.
He poses like a politician,
then swoops through a display
of tactical maneuvers
that rivals the welfare office.

A man asks us where the elephants are.
Then he asks us what they said.
This zoo is a refuge for the truly lost.
They come here with their bread crumbs
and thermoses of muscatel
to do their self-appointed rounds.
An old lady shakes her head
and chastises Billy the Chimp.
He is acting out his adolescence
by beating on the females in his cage.
They cower before him,
pick his fleas and try to be charming.
They know how things go.

Near the Cat House we see a woman
whose torn nylons run up her legs like scars.
We follow her inside where the big black cats
loll in cages and lick their balls.
She yells to everyone that there are flowers
falling from the iron bars that separate us
from the pure white teeth of the cats.
But they are really only roaches,
thousands of legs jerking in a death dance,
poisoned by the keeper who walks
up and down the aisle of cells
squirting his generosity into
every crack and corner.

MIDNIGHT IN THE KANSAS CITY BUS STATION

Two tattooed, leather men attack
the inarticulate cigarette machine.
They have it upsidedown,
plunging and kicking like mustangs.
But she is a tight-fisted woman
and will not yield to them.

Here are a pair of lovers.
And here are the screaming babies
with their teenage mothers destined
only for the dead-ended future.
This is the way the poor go,
like falling stars into the black.

In the station cul-de-sac
two Vietnamese hunch patiently
as they have for hundreds of years.
They compose a meal of chips and neon,
finger their ragged timetable,
think themselves lucky
to be here and not there.

AT THE BORDER

for Candy Clayton

Tonight snow falls, the first in weeks.
It has crept up on us, leaving only
the smallest of dog tracks
down the middle of the road.
The children are asleep.
The kitchen table has been cleared.
I stay up and read your letter from Germany,
onionskin full of snow on stone walls
and in the medieval forests. And your poem
with cold lovers and barbed wire in its teeth.

Why is it we have loved
the saddest of men?
What weeping is in us that needs
to be filled again and again
that we might never touch
the bottom of this pain?
Your fatherless son grows hard
in a German kindergarten.
You see young soldiers at the border
of mine fields, searchlights illuminating
a body, the snarling concertina wire.

I touch my pulse to the sore of this letter.
Tomorrow the birds will need feeding.
And there will be children's voices falling

like bits of steel through the day.
But tonight it continues to snow,
silently, as it has for hundreds of years,
each flake pulling the undertow of history,
the black machine-gun turret, the lonely bed,
the deserted road that is now trackless
as it makes its way through the dark.

FINDING POUND IN VENICE

"A blown husk that is finished
but the light sings eternal
a pale flare over marshes
where salt hay whispers to tide's change."

—*Ezra Pound*

Early evening. December.
I do not want to return just yet
to solitude and the long slippery dark
that approaches from the sea.
In this gloom one wrong step
would take me through the drape of fog
and into the sleep of a dark canal
where I would dream until spring
with the crab and the squid.
In the cafe the thoughtful proprietor
tunes in Bach and turns to his daily paper.
Bottles of wine sigh against the wall.

You sit at the corner table,
too impossibly old, and gently cough,
the tide rising, falling.
A glass of Valpolicella burns
blood-color before you.
From the walls the masks of Venice
reveal everything.
You have worn them all.
Now you are beyond them,
beyond the wine,
and in truth, beyond Bach
and the water of sound which carries
down the distance of the Grand Canal.

All the tortures done with,
you have let go
of reason and madness together.
They never were enough.
In their place you find the wide piazza of death
where mist climbs the walls like cheesecloth.
You rise to go,
a dark man passing over bridges,
away from the Campanile where bells toll the Angelus,
toward the mist where only the initiated
can distinguish sea from air
from safe walk home.

BALGILLOW ISLAND

for Kathy and Fred Doty

I

On Balgillow Island a loon's cry echoes
against the hard forehead of rock.
Fred sands the natural wood.
He will make an altar of shelves
for lifejackets and fishing tackle,
for rusted cans of saved nails and screws,
for notches of saws and those tongues
of wedges that split open
the unquestioning trees.
Birch bark drifts down to pine needles,
curled wreaths of it for spinning.
The lake remains unbroken
by cloud or thought,
covered by a quilt of water lilies
that open to a spawning sky.

II

Lake and trees sturdy in their solitude.
Just before dark, last light on the water
makes a cool blue, and some dark wings,
pairs of pairs of wings flit
through sun going, moon coming.
The isolated whine of motorboat.
In the woods a soft sound
of the invisible.
All things settling,
loons into their dark voices,
mats of moss and pine needles,
bright red and sulphur-lemon mushrooms
in which dew pools,
little bowls of honey and light.

III

I swim briefly among clam shells
and the soft pine needles of lake bed
and through a school of minnows
that parts as if of one mind, one body
for my whiteness to go through.
Riffling of water and flutter of moth wing.
It is late.
The power boats have all gone home.
One child's voice rises from the opposite shore,
one voice above all the others
in its archipelago of joy,
echoing through this labyrinth of water,
lake-chains, one mouth winding into another,
where it is easy to be lost
unless you know the way.

JANUARY, MINNESOTA, 1989

The snow piles down outside,
glistening and crackling.
It's like electric flakes.
Or like crazy high-wire artists
who have had too much of the circus
and plummet to the sawdusted center ring.

This snow does not love
nuclear missiles.
This snow with its grainy fizz
does not like the President
and the Prime Minister,
does not love any of those
who sit above the snow
in the service of capital gain.

But what does the snow know?
It just goes on and on
loving the quiet lovers
who walk their alley-ways tonight.
Loving those who sleep
huddled by our trash cans.
Loving the children who run
their red sleds up and down
its grainy face.

The snow knows that it doesn't take
a lot of practice or learning
to love someone.

You just sit down and do it,
knees touching knees,
foreheads glowing.
The snow knows that tomorrow
all the birds will wake and sing
because we're all still here,
still going into the snow.

Snow on the TV. Snow on
the coveralled one hitchhiking
by the side of the superhighway,
his shoulders blanketed with snow.
And the poor, crazy ones
huddled in their own bright dormitory
for the insane.
Even there it snows,
across their fiery eyes,
across their hands,
and into their hearts that are so full,
that beat like the bells of a Tibetan monastery
calling everyone to prayer
on the mountain covered with snow.

HEISENBERG'S UNCERTAINTY PRINCIPLE

"We must resign ourselves to an inability to predict the vast majority of phenomena . . . and to a reality that is beyond what we observe.
—*Gordon Reece,*
In Praise of Uncertainty

for Bridgit

Midnight,
middle of Ohio,
interstate, fields, and only
the furthest lights
except for the car's highbeams
which throttle on constantly west.
In the back seat my children
keep each other awake
with physics and philosophy.
The younger questions, his voice
thrown steady as a sinker
into the night.
Bridgit answers,
comfortably sure of
the unsureness of it all,
invokes Heisenberg,
talks quarks and atoms,
says we cannot know, cannot know.

Outside the tight mass of our car
old bones resurrect
in the loam of country graveyards.
This is the universe,

all of it,
matter and anti-matter,
the momentum of love zinging
through a damp summer night,
one finger on the world of probabilities,
the other pensively encircling
some elusive face.

What do we know?
Tree, rock, clod of earth.
Creosoted power pole.
The car, the road, our own bodies—
each separated from the other
by only the merest of grace.
Nothing is sure but it is probable
that we will see Wisconsin by dawn,
that the sun will rise dependable
and generous in the east,
that my children will finally sleep,
the white lines on asphalt
like two arms
between which we go.

III

TO FREE THEM ALL

RAISING LAMBS

for Ron and Ann Gower

The lambs push their honey-lips into the grass.
Each one wears a dangly red earring
that tells us shots have been given,
balls castrated,
that the long arm of ownership
has clamped its staple.
They are so small against the spring,
three of them clustered
on a field of green baize
like card players who care more
for companionship than the win or loss.
Black on soft noses,
sooty legs lost in grass.
These are the no-name sheep,
wethers going in a mud-scented June evening
toward their short plump existence.

We move into the house and have lamb for dinner.
Succulent, smeared with mint and garlic,
rainbows of juice in the pockets of our cheeks.
What a fine testimony to this grass, this earth,
to these nursery rhyme loves who will never know
how we have each wished under a full summer moon
to fall on all fours and tear the grass,
to lap water from a cold stone trough,
and to live frivolous all through one summer
before marching full-blooded, red-hearted into fall
toward the butcher's swing of steel,
his unfailing arms which embrace,
take hold and love us
until we know none of it anymore.

MY FATHER'S LAST GAME

Today your old golf clubs arrived
with your ghost at my front door.
The date of the last game you ever played
was stamped in pale red
on the ticket tied to the strap.
I saw how you must have hoisted the bag
over your shoulder, setting out tired
and by then not loving it much.
The ticket says: 18 Holes, South Pine Creek Park.
It warns: Always keep in sight.
And: Good only on the date issued.

My son finds in a pocket of the bag
a bandaid kept for blisters
and a split, black driving glove,
such very small things.
But nothing could protect you by then,
the truth of sun in your eyes,
the trees staggering farther and farther away
as you stepped off the green.

What kind of day was it?
I want to think a white gauze cloud day,
a few birds, you out there alone,
and the ball going where you wanted it to go.
My son says he has never seen a sand wedge,
studies it, rubs its chip marks.
He knows this is the club for difficult places,
for the ball that will elude you,
your strokes slipping down between grains of sand.

IN MY MOTHER'S GARDEN

I

Sunday in my mother's garden.
The dew rises off the lawn
and churchbells clang out
their call to all the faithful.

Here we are faithful only to our childhood,
the sunburned shoulders,
the sand of Jennings Beach rough
between our toes.

But there is an infiltrator in the garden.
We grow old.
My brother wakes up late, eats,
then reads the paper.

We are here together again,
children brought home to their old rooms
by the ambulance siren,
by the inevitable midnight phone call.

The mind had fooled us into complacency
with its railroad circuits that went
round and round a living room,
under couch legs, behind chairs.

The little train of life with its log car dumping
and whistle blowing and the small puffs of smoke
rising like prayers all through a Sunday afternoon.
We thought it would never stop.

Across town our mother sleeps in her austere hospital room.
In her house everything is still
except the old voices echoing
from the mouths of photos on the walls.

II

Today in the hospital room I listened
but I did not hear her pray.
Only yesterday when no one could wake her
did she pray, mumbling in her sleep.

The fragile voice coming from some deep place.
"Holy Mary, Mother of God,
pray for us sinners, now,
and at the hour of our death. Amen."

"Now and at the hour of my death."
Over and over. A drumroll.
Artillery fire.
Wind, cyclone wind.

She stepped up to the house of death
and then came back. Came back scared.
And came back angry because
I had taken too long to get here.

Because I had ever left at all.
Because I had another life,
the angry mother striking out,
the child recoiling, head snapping back.

My feet turn, start to run.
But it is too late for this.
And tonight it is also too late to call,
and so I send my love across the city.

Across all the grimy streets, past the taverns
with their doors open to the early September night.
Across the smokestacks of the General Electric Plant
and past the one lonely elephant in the Bridgeport Zoo.

I think my love all the way up the hill
where two hospital towers rise like stunted arms,
where the lights in rooms go out slowly one by one.
All sleep now. All sleep.

EVOLUTION

"When elephants encounter the skeleton of an elephant out in the open they methodically take up each of the bones and distribute them, in a ponderous ceremony, over the neighboring acres."

—*Lewis Thomas,*
The Lives of Cell

Dusk swings down its censer,
purifying fields, opening up
the road to night.
Along the Minnesota River,
short hills stumble,
push themselves against the rise,
like elephant backs rumbling north,
tail to tail, as if there was
no other direction possible.

On this old river road that bends,
then shoots away straight,
a man was killed,
his truck run head-on
into the oncoming light.
He had no time to fight
or prepare for this leaving.
He let go of his land,
of the creek-bed imprinted
with his desires.
He let go of the grapevines
and the gooseberry bushes
barbed through his memory.

And the elephants lumbered on,
not complaining, as if their
only wish was to spread the bones
of the dead, to distribute them
away from the throbbing compass.
And then to die themselves,
to have no more of wanting,
of waiting behind the tough grey hide,
the fence of tusks guarding
their lonely cheeks.

AFTER A DEATH

Your death recedes like a bad storm,
a sudden one with boiling clouds
the color of ash
that roll out to sea
across water which turns from turquoise
to ink
to blue-green again.

For weeks after you were gone,
you were my first thought on waking,
the mother who had left me where I stood
abandoned on the beach
looking out over a sea where
white gulls circled and cried.
Each day I swallowed that knowing
first breath of morning,
my body snapping in a whiplash.
And then the painful pull away,
the way the placenta tears from the mother
to make two labors, two births.

But today your absence
plays a softer melody.
Colors of morning blend together
in yellow and white.
It is spring.

A cat jumps to the window
to watch the hungry sparrows
which are you now.
The cat. The birds. The morning sun.
It's all you.
And this sky, cloudless,
your high forehead stretched,
wrapping its blue around everything.

The Unread Book

It comes toward you when you least suspect it. You are on a busy street in a foreign country and no one is smiling and you are unsure of the language and the clouds are grey and from every direction mothers push children in strollers who are all crying because they are hungry or bored or sad and you step into a bookshop because it has finally just begun to rain very lightly and you see the unread book you gave your mother the Christmas before she died and you walk over and crack its spine.

THE DEER

It's eight o'clock on a sunny morning. I'm following the yellow dashes down the country road, going to work, not happy about it, imagining all the possibilities narrowing to that dot where the road disappears at the horizon.

Squadrons of blackbirds fly over the car. And then I see the deer, five of them, in the field to my right. They are heading toward the road to cross it. They look young, but I am not a hunter, so I can't really tell how old they are, if they're does or fawns or something else. All of them are running and leaping toward the two-lane country road.

The field they run through is muddy and so the deer seem to lurch and stumble and do not have the gracefulness we expect of them. And they are ragged looking, the same dull color of the fields, a worn color, a wheat color. They're shedding winter coats and tufts of dead fur fly off as they run toward the road.

Suddenly a car appears coming the other way. The deer have gone behind a little knoll. And then they are out on the gravel shoulder. I honk my horn to warn the other driver to see them and stop as I have. He does and four of them leap onto the road, and then across and into the field on the other side. But the fifth one has balked, maybe at the noise of my horn, and does not cross the road but turns and goes back into the field where it stops and looks toward me. Then it looks across the road to where the other deer are out of sight.

There is silence as we wait—the deer, the other driver, and I. Then the deer begins to gallop toward the road, and without hesitating, bounds over it, and races into the moldy field. It gets halfway across, then stops running and turns and looks back. The other driver and I start up our cars and as we approach each other he tips two fingers toward me in the customary country greeting. In the field, bones of plowed-under cornstalks stick up. I suddenly think of my mother, dead years ago. And I wonder—no—I know that you are here.

In Orlando

Arms of steam rise from the tomb of the heated pool.
Darkness has settled between wet stones of the patio,
around the stubborn straight trunks of palms.
Orderly stars clump overhead and far off
the lighted towers of other hotels
circle through their own astronomy.

Here the white shapes of someone else's children
illuminate a make-believe green lagoon.
Their father swims with them,
heavy in their wake.
He lumbers back and forth in the placid pool
out of heart-breath and mind-breath.
What is it that pulls this man down,
away from his children who squeal
like the soft tires of a brand-new car?

In the darkness he could be my father, dead fifteen years.
I imagine his familiar sunburned shoulders, pink flesh
peeking out through freckled skin.
He wears his old Marine ID bracelet
and the green nylon quick-drying swim trunks
my mother bought him for Father's Day.
He will die too soon, although
I did not know this, never guessed.
And it will be painful and long,
his only relief from the cancer
to float on his back in our neighbor's small pool.

Here in Orlando this is just another
inconsequential evening,
the clean smell of chlorine in the damp air,
and the soft underwater lights of the pool
shimmering on the surface.
As it darkens, I imagine
my brother and I are young again.
We're in the pool,
swimming around my father like polliwogs,
underwater, holding onto him,
letting go. We want to play
"Break the Old Lady's Chair."
And so once again he plants his legs
like two pilings.
And back bending, he scoops us up,
one at a time, and tosses us a fathom away,
the life-line between us stretched,
then tested, then broken.

POEM BEFORE SLEEPING

"The space between our fingers . . . is a memorial to cells that die, for otherwise we would have webbed fingers."

—Theoretical Aspects of Developmental Biology

Before sleeping the cat cleans herself.
She licks, then scratches
under her morsel of chin.
She pays long attention
to the small dark spaces between her nails.
The world has stuck there.
Chipmunk fur. Tree bark. Sparrow feathers.

She looks up suddenly and purrs,
then goes back to the ritual washing,
a sacrament of fur and whiskers.
She ignores the weighty books
which someone has left around her body.
When she is finished cleaning
she curls her head down
in between her paws.

But this cat has left dark intestines
freezing at the front door
and old bones cracked and scattered
across the backyard.
Floating toward the waters of sleep
she does not remember anything
of hunting now. The sparrows
scared up from their dry bushes,
mice blurred in a race of tears.

DEAD MEN'S CLOTHES

I have come here where I think there are no memories,
no dark well of water in which to drown.

But in your closet I see my father's tie,
the red and navy one I gave him when I was 20,

shopping in New York at Brooks Brothers,
trying to love him and not knowing how.

He scolded me, dismissed the gift as extravagant,
then wore it. This was his way of loving me.

I can see you haven't worn the tie yet.
It is only a dead man's tie, frayed and faded,

the stripes exhausted in their narrow trenches.
I reach to throw it out.

It doesn't work to try to keep our past alive like this,
to hold our memories like babies close to our chests.

They wear out and escape us,
turning and tumbling into a world we don't control.

Like strident children they get away,
insist on being abandoned.

They won't lie still for comforting,
don't bring any softness to our old age.

I see you have other dead men's things here:
An ex-girlfriend's father's suit,
your own silent father's watch.

All these hand-me-downs as if our lives
really were one continuous trajectory.

To the incinerator with it all.
To the metal heart of the city dumpster.

Let them lie there together,
all the dead fathers waiting for the strike of match,
waiting for the liberating flame.

THE BIRD RELEASE AT THE MINNESOTA LANDSCAPE ARBORETUM

I watch the flocks of children,
charge up, turn,
then roll lopsided
down the green bowl of hill.
None of them are mine.
Some drag dead branches around
or carry the single daffodil
they were told not to pick.
Their parents clutch cameras
and discarded mittens.
The Sunday clouds mass over our heads
and it is too cold for the end of April.

The birds are in cardboard boxes
clustered like a bivouac
at the bottom of the hill.
There are hawks whose wings were broken.
Owls that learned the truth
of a semi's headlights.
Falcons who believed their territory
was the whole unrolled bolt sky
before they met the grid of power lines.

They have all been healed
and taught to fly again.
Now they wait in darkness
while talk goes on around them.
They are thinking field mouse, gopher, snake,

oil spill, steel trap,
the breath of the invisible glass.
If they're lucky they'll live,
find mates, build nests,
and raise their young in the sanctuary
of this second chance.

Above us buds are just beginning
to filigree the green-tipped trees.
Sun breaks through the clouds
and parents gather their children.
The bird releasers put on big, thick gloves.
Now their hands are like the declawed paws
of large and clumsy cats.
One by one they wrestle each bird out of its box,
then climb up and stand on a picnic table.
We all count—ONE, TWO,
and on THREE the releasers
open their hands and give their bird
a boost up into the sky
like a handful of confetti.
It's an explosion of wings.
We don't know which way they will go.
People clap and cheer.
Then we're silent as each bird does
what it knows best.
It flies away from us,
the Great Horned Owl going

low and serious right over my head,
climbing higher and higher,
through the trees,
under the wires,
over the marsh and then gone.
It only takes a little while to free them all.

CARY WATERMAN was born in Connecticut, has lived in Colorado, New Mexico, and Minnesota, and is the mother of three children. She has degrees from the University of Denver and Mankato State University.

Her books of poems include, *The Salamander Migration*, *First Thaw*, and *Dark Lights the Tiger's Tail*. She co-edited, with Jim Moore, the anthology, *Minnesota Writers: Poetry*. Her own poems appear in many anthologies including, *A Geography of Poets*, *Woman Poet: The Midwest*, and *The Decade Dance*. She has spent time at the MacDowell Colony and at the Tyrone Guthrie Centre in Ireland. Her writing awards include two Bush Foundation Fellowships, a Minnesota State Arts Board Fellowship, the Loft-McKnight Award, and the Loft-McKnight Award of Distinction in Poetry.

Cary Waterman teaches writing courses at Augsburg College , The Loft, and Metropolitan State University. She is also a coordinator with Student Support Services at Normandale Community College.